AF265928

My BEST Year Yet!

JoshuaTreePublishers
Copyright @ 2019 by JoshuaTreePublishers.
All rights reserved.